Ways to Stay Miserable
Politics of Melancholy versus Happiness

Roma Desai

PublishAmerica
Baltimore

ISBN: 1-4137-4537-7
PUBLISHED BY PUBLISHAMERICA, LLLP
www.publishamerica.com
Baltimore

Printed in the United States of America

For Nihar

Acknowledgements

To my father and mother I owe everything for giving me the opportunities I have had in life, for showing me a purposive and responsible mode of human life. My principle thanks must be to my brother; he was the person who enjoyed my story-telling sessions in our early childhood years.

Last, but by no means least, for their encouragement, support and love, I would thank my father-in-law and mother-in-law.

But my most sincere thanks of all are for Nihar. For his patience, I title him with all respect.

My special thanks must be to members of PublishAmerica, who offered me most valuable advice and unfailing support.

In the hours between dawn and dusk:

Dawn

But it's dawn, and here is a brief account of the grinding misery that inspired everything in my life. Life has many interesting features, and most critical is the behaviour of the mind states. The need to build myself up is probably what makes me look deep, at my drill and ways to stay miserable.

One specific mind state that I want to talk about is what you in a world of thoughts and feelings call "melancholy," which is a very deep feeling of sadness, and I am captivated by melancholy. I think melancholy is a wake-up call for the person's attention; it is an attitude marked by a paradoxical mood of realism.

I think my life has been a bunch of miseries to work with.

The sun is already high.

I think I am tired of my situation, but I am really tired of my thoughts. I wake up feeling miserable, and I do not want to stay miserable. I look back on my life, things that I wanted to do or be or could have had.

I think about ways to get out of this whirlpool of the miserable feeling, and I go around in circles unendingly. One thing leads to another; the thoughts flash from beginning to finish almost in a chorus and also in many directions. I can now see that the nearness of melancholy is distracting.

I realise that attitude of happiness is in the present, "here and now," and not somewhere else or in the near future. That's how I rationalise making a choice.

The mind begins to breed images and thoughts of what my eyes ought to see. I kick and I wriggle to hold and to capture firmly my thoughts of passion and desires and each time I sense only the presence of a condescending sneer. I sit up blind. *Who is meeting today, and what are they talking about?* I can't help wondering.

I sit up, and I stare for hours and reminisce over and over about events of last night or the previous day and the reasons why I need to snap out of this "miserable feeling." I am, as the saying goes, "burned out."

Quite quickly, but then again, hopeful messages pop up and dance about; a part of me wants to pick these up and walk away. I take it that my mind is just making yet one more attempt to distract attention from the truth. I guess that my mind is pretty good at generating new ideas and breeding images regarding different ways to beat this melancholic feeling. It feels kind of "sexy"!

"I am feeling pretty tired of my thoughts," I admit. I often feel trapped by my feelings. My feelings are ever so changeable, and I know that I can have a hand in changing them. This is the "one thought" that has sustained me throughout the years.

"Beat it now!" I find that my fight to "beat it" is invariable; instead, my thoughts navigate me towards the most tiresome attitude, which is "staying miserable." I ask myself, "Why can't things be easy? Why can't I be happy—just for a day?"

A funny "just one day," I must have said this so many times in my lifetime so far. I have now drained all of my emotions, and I feel exasperated. I forget the times that I have been happy, and it does not take me long to snap out of happiness mainly for the excuses that I offer myself.

I remind myself of the reality, emotional reality of what happened in the past or what may happen as a consequence of my decision to relax or step back today.

I know that I need to exist as an individual, to do and not keep thinking "what to do?" and see melancholy "what more is there." I know too well what it is that I am criticising in my life.

I decide "what I want."

The fears and my excuses consume my happiness as a whole, and I feel bad feeling miserable. My heart begins to pound. I talk to myself endlessly, balancing the reasons for my existence and whether or not my life is worth it or "what I get is what I deserve."

It is ever so easy to stay miserable while the happiness swirls around at the rim. On the other hand, I seem convinced that there is no way that I deserve to stay miserable; I deserve to celebrate every moment and live life to the full. My search for excuses begins with "but why?"

I think, I know, and I believe that I need to detach myself and learn to take responsibility for my own actions, and yet again the "but" returns. I feel compelled to explain everything; I feel the fear, and part of the reason may be that my many views and feelings are stuck in the layers of past experiences including the present ones.

When I think about the future, I am afraid of getting something that may afterwards be taken away. I think of an expression, "you don't get owt for nowt."

I acknowledge my experiences, and I think it is important to take away from them the aspects that I want to keep. Melancholy does not merit an embrace; I need not hang on to my tired thoughts; I cannot tell, but I feel some connection. Melancholy always feels so close, and happiness far-off, often beyond my reach.

I might be naïve to think that I can just look for happiness and knock off the gloomy feelings. I think that my feeling of despair is my own creation, mainly because I have removed my desire to be an individual from my mind and put it in my new wretched role for everyone's use.

I search among my fears and excuses, and this suggests to me that I am searching for something and do not find it.

It is not difficult to crush my feelings of hopes all together and brood over life's injustices. I can find many ways to "stay miserable." I feel unsatisfied, so I select a misery option to resist the happiness that I may achieve in the future. While all of these thoughts and feelings are going through my mind, I am also trying to get ready for work, listening to the daily morning news, analysing and criticising the government policies.

I have had a quick shower, prepared and eaten my breakfast, glanced through my appointments for the day, as well as written a couple of notes to myself and stuck these on my computer desk. "How distant or detached is that?"

I am extremely busy, hopping from one bus to another, as

well as being fully aware of the happenings on the street corners and the people around me; my mind continues to breed new images.

Breeding images and thoughts are confining when I need to recognise the happiness.

I react to thoughts linked to gruesome frustrations, desperate thoughts on a desperate day. I think about whether or not I could have done any better and if only I could've had a chance. I have to ask myself, "what chance might that be?"

I must give myself a chance to experience and be willing to see what comes out of it. To get the clues I have to look at myself and not at what might have been. The need to "trust myself wholly," is probably what makes me doubt myself in such an excessive manner.

It is time to pay attention to my appointments. I put my thoughts on hold, and I carry on with the day-to-day routine and work, even though my breeding thoughts and images remain very much at the brim of my eyelids. I start with shuffling the paper work and writing my notes. I have learned to shove my specific feelings into the little boxes mainly because they have a disconcerting habit of popping up in my mind for a lift up time and again.

Sometimes "to do nothing" is to continue running.

Sonny tried to get me to talk about work, my day and the related events. I usually cut the topic short, but I don't know what there was inside me that I started to talk about my work and the recent events.

I noticed his downbeat responsiveness, although he remained polite and kind. This put me back into the sulky mood; I resorted to my tiresome zone, "the miserable feeling." There is nothing I could do but dismiss his attitude of indifference.

I decide that I will not do any explaining or tell anymore; I find out that I no longer have words to describe my shock and my response at this juncture. I am also least likely to plan what I can do next with my thoughts and feelings.

Okay, so everything has brought my hopeful thoughts to a screeching halt, the feelings that I put up there and rounded up together. I see that my melancholic feeling does not come from Sonny's disconcerting response but from trying to work out why he asked, "How are you?"

I decide to take the view that he is responding to his thoughts and feelings, not my being.

I begin to mull over a number of things quietly as well as continue with my daily tasks. I have completed so many assignments and worked for this organisation for a couple of years now.

I think the manager likes my work, at least that is how it appeared, but more recently, he seems distant. I don't know what to make of this; my confidence is marred, as he is sulky and contrary where his mood is concerned. I think it is my anxiety that tells me that I am not at rest. I reckon that he is feeling pressured due to staff shortage or possibly has other organisational matters to deal with.

I also know that from the very start something about my general appearance has always annoyed the other senior manager. There are about 50 employees in the team, but I am among the select handful of those whose aspect he couldn't always put up with.

However, this was hardly new to me. I cannot tell what it is that is happening with my manager now. I am experiencing a variety of feelings and thoughts, and I do not want to see so many negative feelings inside me. Now I can't even talk about this issue; it has suddenly become a sore point in my mind and interactions. "How scary is that?"

I know that I will not always have the protection that I need, to help towards preventing the breeding images and thoughts from reappearing and popping up in so many new forms.

The only way for me to make contact with this manager is to leave him with his experiences, not think about him. I need to stop talking to myself and thinking that I have done something wrong.

I have often been too quick to accept anything as my failing. My experience has shown me that, when I have acknowledged my mistakes, I have learned. I am a relationship, changeable with circumstances and at different life stages.

While my thoughts and feelings of my failings were ebbing away, I started to flow with life, and I kind of liked the flow of experience. It is my feeling that my fault is not tolerable by others that they see me through the results not my attempts.

I just need to feel at ease, need to understand my thoughts and actions and their meaning; I feel that I am potentially unable to do well mainly because of the way that others see me. Life sometimes seems absolutely peculiar, and as I continue to feel miserable, there are also a few hidden ecstatic aspects of my life.

I look from the window of my mind, from the inside out; I see birds and hear all sorts of noises and distortions in the air, but I do not hear the one that triggered my unhelpful thoughts. I heard a lot of them with radical differences at least half a dozen times before.

I have no disagreements with anyone, everything always seems possible, and yet no thought seems to stay linked with me for long. The mind has a way of designing many new strategies and combines well with every little thing in my life and continues breeding riff-raff images of sorts time after time.

I accept my faults, and I think there is no virtue in reacting to criticisms with hurt feelings. I will most certainly see it as a new learning.

On the face of things, my family members are polite and gentle as well as kind. Their emotional tactics send the shockwaves through me, and they remind me of the tensions rather than my actions. I am forever explaining, and everything always seems so complicated. I am always responding to the comments of my family members that "I am too sensitive."

I feel, I have been wasting time. I possibly cannot hack it and thus feel angered. I think that I have not failed, just haven't made it to the top or reached the medium zone. I believe that I have nearly touched it, and it has not been that bad. I have to get a grip; I need to be positive and not disregard my abilities.

I am ever changing, going from one decision to the next, thinking each one is for keeps.

I must accept that sometimes situations can be beyond

one's control and everything does not go as planned. Sometimes my interactions with people are hopeless and frustrating. I do not like some people while I know that everyone else in my family does.

When I am being angry, my family seems to readily stick their attention to my words rather than to my feelings and thoughts. The question: "where does all this politics of family life originate from?" I was doing fine in the morning, and in fact, I had a nice, relaxed break, completed most of the tasks and was feeling rested. Now, the reason is clear. I had time to listen to my feelings.

This suggests to me that I want for my family to like me. My anxiety does not come from thinking about the way I should be liked but from having this deep need within me for wanting us to be close. I want to be able to talk to them.

I think, I am disappointed at what I have experienced so far, and today I want to feel life, want a life; I want it sooner rather than later; I want it "here and now." It is striking as to how easily the down in the dumps feelings can home in on my "self."

These feelings are here to stay, in that there is hurt and pain, and it runs through my life, comes in waves and pops up time and again.

I know that my kith and kin have expectations of me to do well, and I try, I truly try, and at times feel exasperated. In my distressed moments, I sometimes strike my efforts and fail to appreciate my trying.

I need reminding; I conclude that I cannot live by expectations, but I can make the grade by appreciating my trying. It is "I" that matters, and I must recognise this.

I am certain that I do not have to consult the politics of family life to know how happy I can feel "here and now." My struggle with today is to respond to tensions between "what I should be" and "what I am." I can choose, I always can.

Deep within, I know that happiness and my relationship with nature is imminent. It starts as a rather tricky "search," and most critical and novel about this relationship is the idea of finding in myself the willingness to like my "self." I have tried to stay distant from specific feelings and thoughts, and I am usually able to access the escape to solitude and fantasy.

My associates, Judith and Marilyn, tell me to get a life the whole time; they suggest that I must meet people and go to book clubs or to meet up at the coffee shop and enjoy chitchat. I instantly strike such suggestions. As for me, it is a tall order, and it causes me immense unease.

I don't exist so I can be liked. I like my solitude, and I have with me these feelings of melancholia and pleasurable moments, which home together. I look to the brief images from the various stages of my life searching for some answers. It gives me strength, a cheerful swing and a tilt as well as adds on a few colours of harmony to my life.

I decide that solitude is a profound feeling of freedom and proper recognition of self-love and self-appreciation.

The need to build myself up is probably what makes me want to understand the politics of family life. I am usually able to call upon a few tangled sets of memories, both joyful and excruciatingly painful from my relationships.

My thoughts are like flock of birds going around above the city. I do not lead the way, and I admit that my memories are not always a good guide to set clear boundaries; rather, I have very often and most easily been influenced by the occasional soft manner of others or the callous mocking by my thoughts and memories of others doing the same.

My despair is that I always explain and say so little; humiliation is rather like an incessant tune of my life. I am always the one to go down on my knees for freedom from strife, which is usually without much success.

I am a relationship always trying every which way to make contact with the other person. If I feel duty-bound to explain every aspect of my feeling, I am the one forcing the attitude of sufferer inside me.

Sonny tried and conveniently knitted into his stories, convoluted the real situations to blame me for his downfall. I feel disgust, and honestly, sometimes "I am not even bothered." He seems like someone who has stepped on every feeling that I have ever felt.

I know that Sonny and Hilda show signs of feelings for me, and they have also incessantly ground me to non-existence. This has happened on many occasions and almost through many years and far too many times. I have kicked and wriggled in frustration, felt like a worm, endeavoured to express and resolve or look for solutions, but everything that I have ever said or done has fallen on deaf ears. "How cruel can the power of family be, eh?"

I moan and I express amusement and endure being emotionally ablaze; my tears most certainly will provide a cascade of my experiences. Like clouds, I am so absolutely uninhabited. I continue to smile and occasionally cry tears of fear and pain simply because I care.

I think, in a genuine relationship, show of affection is not about saying nice things to people or doing the right things. I am a relationship ever so grateful that I am into life; sometimes the question, "what to do?" is to continue denying.

Sonny and Hilda do not think or feel like me, and that's not wrong either.

Being polite and gentle to others is in essence my personality, and I believe I am wary too. However, a friend Bradley Black is in need. He requires help, and this is where it all began. I provided shelter, quiet moment and a breathing space to him, and that I should have never left for him to prey.

Generally an unexpected happened, and the sunshine and good deed began to turn hazy. My good deed did not go down well. I should have known better, and now it's getting taxing, and I feel totally and pretty much on my own with my view of people. I feel such a "perfect fool"!

I am just beginning to fish for criticisms that I am so used to. Maybe I have forgotten to respect my ability to patrol my life. I just don't seem to have got anything through my thick skull.

I have been feeling anxious about my decision; my life is a mix of unresolved problems. "What was I thinking?" I have no thoughts in the matter. It is generally nice to giggle with my husband, and we haven't had a laugh or a giggle since Bradley's arrival. It's been ages; it's like a time warp; everything has changed. I feel exhausted; I have had a long day.

I am experiencing a mixture of feelings. I have been kidding myself. What I am saying is that, if Bradley stays, "nobody is going to be dancing tonight." Hence, it's fine for me to go down the melancholic lane and say one more "goodnight," or better, I must ask him to leave.

I feel like kicking myself when I see Bradley living like a lord in my home. It isn't always a question of your attitude towards the other person. Quite often what counts is their attitude towards you. Right now this annoyance is my reality. I tried to help Bradley and couldn't.

When I accept my sincerity, I no longer see it as an error of judgement on my part.

I tried to talk it out. I also decided to write myself a note about yet another family drama. I must say that it is a little different from my previous tone. I am not having a very good time. I don't want to tear myself apart over this issue. I need to clear my head as this new melancholy has worn all of us out; Bradley has disrupted our family.

I am sure that I will find an answer and at the best appropriate time. This episode is beginning to look a sort of nasty, "sure it does"! I start to take a calculated guess about the politics of family life and social interactions. I realise that there has been a miscalculation. This miscalculation was mine, of course.

My fears and lack of faith in human nature is a constant disappointment to me. I try to give my actions their possible meaning based on my experiences.

It is no secret that I can't see eye to eye with Bradley Black, and I am trying to do fine, being gentle and polite. I wonder, *What was I thinking?*

I can think stronger than that, and yet I refrain mainly because I want to believe that my observations might be simply subjective, although I know my instincts are true to the core. During all these years, I maintained a clear head; I knew how to make things right, and I knew and saw the split in people.

My word, I can no longer stand a falter. I didn't know that I could hate so much; that's why I have to be true to how I feel and what I believe. I am carrying a terrible burden; I am so "sorry."

I have made a terrible mess of things, and while I tried to do the right thing, our friend Bradley Black took it the wrong way. He is just like yesterday's newspaper; he is the essence of disruption.

I think that I might possibly be foolish to be too trusting of other people, which suggests to me that if I am not careful, I will regret my actions. Through experiences, I am learning. The choice of responding to the different levels of my feelings is up to me and not in the hands of Bradley Black.

I have had issues with my family for a long time, and while these stand unresolved, I am stuck with Bradley Black, who has marital and financial problems, and he is trying to home in on my space and my life.

I am sounding like a one-woman band, suggesting ways to be unhelpful and rid Bradley Black of the quiet space that I so helpfully provided him. At least I know what is important, and I may ask him to leave, consider change of gears. I have so much more to take care of, especially myself, and although it may feel a little sleazy, discord needs seeing from the close range, even though it might feel like I have turned into a villain. I understand nothing beyond the fact that I cannot help Bradley.

This is the guy; I sincerely hope he would tell me what he was thinking when he decided to home in on my freedom in my idyllic retreat, which is "my home."

His seduction means suggest that he is rude and he is a bully. If I do not act now, I believe that I will be as inconsiderate as Bradley Black.

Middle of the Day

My anxiety often comes from thinking about the future, "what next?" It is usually the tension between "what I should be" and "what I am." Yesterday, I tried unveiling my own expectations. I really did. I chose a whole new set of hopes, and I wanted to change the tunes.

The reason was simply that I wanted to rely on myself and see—what is there in me that I don't want my husband to see? I never believed that the use of any colourful lacy lingerie created by the famous designers would transform the way that he would speak to me, love me or listen to me and enjoy everything that I have to offer.

I do not like the way that I started to consider the strength of pleasurable materials, what I felt raises the question about "why then do I feel this anxiety to please?" These questions acknowledge what matters to us is not the pleasure of making use of the designer products but the connection and the experience of the way that I see our relationship and myself.

I feel, I have got what I have wanted but not enough of what I thought I needed.

To think how so easily I could walk into the melancholic zone, it was kind of another attempt to distract attention from the reality. All I needed to do was to listen to my responses, to the different levels of experiences.

When I have listened to my feelings, I have liked myself better. If I want to feed my soul with happiness and allow my spirits a lift up all over again, then it raises a question on my attitude to melancholy.

Today, I do not want to lose myself, the only way for me to experience his love, not think about my need to feel loved.

The way I see it, melancholy is the "ultimate orgasm." The melancholic flow of experience generates feelings of pleasure and releases the negative energy.

My husband tried to get me to answer, to tell him the reasons "why men, while kissing, slide their hands down toward a woman's bust line and why people close their eyes while kissing."

I had no answer, and I did not want to go along the path of Oedipus complex or anything else. Nothing would've had the unbiased interpretation "in the end." His questions are multiplying as I write. While opening the Amazon parcel, he struck a note for me, which said, "It's easier to undress a woman than a paper parcel."

And I think, *What's his game? What's going on?* Nevertheless these questions acknowledge that there is always a moment when a man experiences himself as "being indispensable," and it is rather "cute"!

In my belief, there is no connection, no matter how deeply you search through brief flirtations with the idea of the candle night parties and Ann Summers events or entertaining thoughts of surgery during the lunch hour. If I want to feel better in myself, then to obsess about the Botox treatment, an opportunity to look prettier or better, is not a solution to my problems; it is not a point on continuity or pleasure and happiness.

For me, these seduction scenes come over me in waves, and I watch these scenes form a cloud before my face and pass. I see the paradox of putting enormous faith in the future while my present itself carries a huge task of loving and liking myself. But I decide to act now.

I decide that I will not address myself as in the third person. I think, I know what it is I am feeling. I can.

Today I want to live, say a lot of things, I want to lose myself in actual experience itself, and what I feel raises the following questions:

"What is melancholy?"

"Why is melancholy a complicating factor?"

"When does melancholy happen?"

"Where does melancholy show?"

"And who feels melancholy?"

I would like to leave the melancholic mood and think no more; I have a good reason to step back and take a break from my dramatic past experiences and the ongoing nervous headaches caused by the politics of family life.

What is right so I don't have to admit my desire for melancholy? I feel pain as well as a joyful moment, and I want the right to consider my present, which is pretty muddled. My future is seemingly vague, combined with a mesh of threadbare relationships that I would like to continue.

I find little things pure and beautiful; I believe that there is beauty in everything that I see, as well as melancholy and joy in every situation.

I feel and I see. No one is wrong. I try to accept what is—I know that is what is required.

When all's said and done, while in the guise of love and care, Sonny and Hilda, in their individual ways, assume control over my feelings, talking me through the ways in which I must think and feel. We have an expression, "Who wants enemies if you have family?"

"Choosing?" I will most certainly not choose between the relationships. I feel that differences in relationships need to be acknowledged. I love and live for all that's true to life. I do not want to act like a part; I would rather acknowledge myself as a person.

I can see that I am not the one Sonny and Hilda assume that "I am" or "I should become." I recognise that I cannot go on living in the fenced areas waiting to be acknowledged for the person that "I am." It is just not enough for me. I'm different.

I am a relationship supposed to do as my family say; they wrap it up unwittingly, plain and simple to their advantage. They claim that they are only trying to save me from anguish of any form. Oh! "How very thoughtful of them?"

I think that it is the threadbare nags within relationships sometimes that bring to the fore the looming melancholic moods. The fleeting apologies coming out of guilt very often lose the meaning while further compounding the confusion embedded already in the relationships.

The way I see it, melancholy emerges from the suppressed feelings, and the wondrous joy emerges from expression known as "freedom." For all its clarity, the understanding of the reasons that cause melancholic moods can briefly remove the anguish and pain. I also know that persistent and consistent nagging relationships cause undeviating low feeling for me, as a result of which I am not particularly spontaneous. I do not act my part, and my true ability so quickly gets submerged.

It is not so difficult to comprehend or even imagine that I hurt by the reinforcement of negativity, for constantly being talked down at. I feel the dreariness, and certainly it does not transform me into an amiable being but into a tedious and an uninteresting being.

If I recognise that my relationships are holding me back through emotional links and they always wriggle out of their responsibilities, I do not have to ask, "what do I want to do?"

Looking to put the blame somewhere is a waste of energy, and sometimes it is like playing a dangerous game. I recognise that I am deeply entrenched in the long-term nagging relationships. I decide to take responsibility for my moods.

In identifying what causes a melancholic feeling is the first step to working through the waste of suppressive relationships. My main thoughts while amongst the many, I feel that there are others who may not have the hope or the freedom to make a similar choice or ability to take responsibility for the way in which they must feel.

Taking responsibility does not mean that I have to take

responsibility for the other person's error or misdemeanour. I need to acknowledge my feeling rather than the other person's action and take responsibility for my own action or role in the matter. I am beginning to acknowledge my role and responsibility and learning new ways to bring about positive changes.

My desires must therefore be in feeling okay and comfortable, combined with the acknowledgement of pain or excellence and of the present.

I know for a fact that we cannot choose our relatives. I think relatives are not always honky-dory, as the nature may have suggested. I decide, I want to stop looking out for a coherent family life.

If I feel that I have a choice as well as freedom, then I don't have to ask "what to do with the freedom." I know for a fact that there are those people who are not able to exercise their choice mainly because of the circumstances in which they live.

If I am privileged enough that I can act upon my free will, I do not need to look from the outside in. I want to look from the inside out.

What I want is to see freedom for everyone as well as that it should not be excepted due to reason of possible failure. I take a view that right to fail allows a chance to new learning.

Happiness does not lie in the success and riches. I can see how, despite being successful, one can feel unhappy, and this might be as a result of the specific norms or formal procedures within our environment and social circles.

I decide to live a life by staying as far away and not in the norms and pressures of the emotional links.

Emotional interaction and willingness to feel the feelings of others, to be able to step back and imagine oneself in other person's situation is a skill to be learned. It allows and sets a platform to un-knot the biases that we may have or agitate us as well as helps to remove the stumbling blocks to happiness.

I take a view that melancholy is not a sign of hopelessness. I believe in its potential for reflection, self-love and respect, coupled with appreciation of oneself and ability. I have a desire to be constructive and to nourish my mind. Melancholic feelings are ever changing, and my experience has shown that these do not stay put for long.

The way I see it, I am different. How I choose to react to my feelings and thoughts is my responsibility.

I remember the times when I was feeling very low and to get by or to understand the way that I was feeling. I was attempting to un-knot the melancholia. I was also feeling the joy of my capacity to take pain, realising that I still had the desire to work with my various thoughts and feelings.

Days of consistent scorn from the loved ones have a way of grinding at the basis, causing a gash little by little. I don't presume even to guess at what they might bring next.

When I provide justifications for the acts of people who consistently disregard me, I believe you will think that I am as thoughtless as the next person, as I never let it come to the only chance and choice that they may have, so they can decide to take responsibility for their actions.

These days of fatigue and despair have taught me all over again that there are no destructive thoughts and feelings, only destructive acts.

The affection for the nearest and dearest does not pass away or cease any day or ever; each day is hard work and painful. I often wonder, and sure enough, this raises a question about the sensitivity and the deep-seated truth about emotional relationships and links with the past.

My experience has shown that things are not always as bad as they might look, and I will most certainly like to consider a way forward, to change the circumstances. I want to quickly get to resolve my situation and stay close to people that I care about. I am also a relationship that needs to take responsibility for self-love and respect.

My love and affection for the other person cannot be under any threat. What I feel simply cannot be taken away from me. Neither does my feeling diminish by stepping back in relationships. I am a person of complete integrity, and I have an opportunity to practise separation from hurtful interactions. There are times I decide to shut my mind to get by, for the way that I feel. I like myself when I am myself, and I care because I want to care.

I think that the ability to achieve one painless day is a combination of two elements—the willingness to allow others to like and dislike me as they choose.

I am certain that my anxiety running through my life is the tension between my deep need for us to be close and a combination of many hurtful interactions. When I accept "what is," I sense a difference, an air of warmth around me and feeling of control, which is what is novel about the melancholia. It's a relationship that dominates my life.

Most experiences imply, life is never so simple and easy, and I do not try to change the feelings of the other people as if they were wrong. From time to time, I want to respect and remember the many moments that have made me stand up to my own scrutiny.

I have ever so often acted as my own severe critic, and especially if things got a little rough for my relationships. I want to experience time to step back and think, take this opportunity to reflect on issues that are most important to me.

The only way for me is not to live my life for approval. I do not have to respond to continuous criticisms and frustrations of others with hurt feelings.

My experience has shown that it is not easy to detach from the emotional links and the people that I care about. This suggests that I have to be true to myself, and if I cannot exist as an individual, then my relationships do not have a meaning.

I want to be able to say anything, and I do not appreciate the way in which the conversations on the other night digressed into unfair criticisms and unhelpful remarks towards me. I feel so ashamed; I feel so messed up; I feel guilty and do not like the way I acted towards Sonny.

I know that I am not at all as bad as what Sonny's comments implied. Years of hurtful comments have shown me time and again that I am terrible at defending the way that I am.

While I want to act out of love and respect for myself, I feel a little fatigue and panic. I want to avoid any form of contention. I begin to ask myself, *What is there in me that brings about negativity in my tone?*

This question and doubt suggests an avoidance of

change that I continue to judge my life by what others say to me. I seem to be fighting a fact rather than dealing with it.

Accept what is, if I want to keep the peace in the home, in relationships and to prevent a heated argument all over again, as well as humiliation in the presence of others.

I don't presume even to guess that it is going to be my deal. I know that I have a choice in the matter, and I do not want to feel hurt again. However troubled that I might feel, I can see and give myself to the possibility that I have ability to diffuse a situation and capacity to work through pain.

I don't always want to be searching for wrongs in me, feeling messed up and guilty. My trouble is that I, until not so long ago, took responsibility for others, fixed my attention on their thoughts and feelings rather than my thoughts and feelings.

I do not exist to be liked, and I do not need to pressure myself into explaining every act on my part, as in so doing, I am the one compelling me into resigning. How everyone else chooses to react is his or her responsibility.

The way for me to live is to stay out of rituals and roles chosen by my emotional links. My purpose is to find approval from within; it is not in the environment or with the others. There is nobody better or more important than I am; I am different, and there are many successful or not so successful people, which is very relative.

I like my difference; I like "what I am." I value and appreciate my virtue of self-love. It began occurring to me that the ability to stay miserable can be replaced with a just one recognisable attitude, which is the desire to feel happiness.

Today, I have a desire to give myself to the attitude of joy. I want to live from the moment of present. Knowing what I can do and want to do, it is vital.

I have learned various ways to respond to the odd details in my own behaviour, and I believe I have been putting blame on myself for the consequences of my acts and taking guilt for everything that might not have gone as planned.

The same things have happened on most occasions. I so easily have let every little feeling of joy slip off merely because I am very good at taking pain, and I am not good at enduring joy in the present.

Days of hugely emotional moments have taught me that I never have let my feelings come to the "choice." I have so easily made use of my capacity to endure pain rather than experience attitude of present, "joy and melancholy."

Time and time again, I have listened to my mind suggesting to me that I can control what happens to me. However, I also have thoughts, which are accompanied by disputable feelings in that I do not think that it can be as simple a case as my mind seems to suggest. I choose to do the opposite of what the mind suggests and try to search out from the coherent phase of emotional links someone that may be able to help control what happens to me.

Little do I try to recognise the despair this sort of an act has caused me before. I am already going through an acute self-doubt phase, starting off again putting people from either the emotional links and present associates in the position of trust and ending up leaving uncertainty in charge of what happens to me.

I seem to have denied the attention and tried not to misread that it has been invariably these same associates and emotional links that are the ones who could not say a word to me without saying the opposite of what they meant.

If I have to ask, "If I can trust," I do not.

I admit that I cannot ignore that I am a relationship, a part of the society and a family and that I have emotional links, and this is what I am presently reviewing. It is not fear of embarrassment; it is an act of relationship that I do not appreciate.

I learned the truth that I cannot change much about my experiences, but I have capacity to endure and capacity to survive pain or failure.

I am on my way out, and since I have decided to feel going backwards as a part of the flow experience, "it's a good life."

Like many, I have tried many new ways to get everything straight and sorted in my head and then the question, "what were you thinking?" After pondering for hours, all over again, I am obstinately determined not to pursue a feel-good factor through the superficial aspects such as, lip enhancement and nose reshaping.

The Botox treatment during the lunch hour does not convince me; self-awareness increases my options, my choices. I feel unable to give myself to claims such as, "I can do what I like, build castles of joy and freedom."

It is enough that I can make a difference now. What I want to do is experience just the one feeling which is freedom and respect for myself.

My experience has shown that freedom is about being flexible and feeling in tune with one's own feelings, which might be joyful or miserable. It is a relationship that I must feel all of the time. Freedom cannot be placed at any extremes mainly because it is an individual experience; it is about free will and choice, individual values and truthfulness to self as well as appreciation of love and care for "I" and "me."

Freedom is a real statement, not a question, and I have a chance to feel and say something. Life is good, when life is freedom and there is much pleasure and joy. I can't leave at this as I think of those who are into severe unfairness and injustices. I know that I am living a life, maybe better than most in many parts of the world, and their thoughts leave me cold and miserable.

I don't presume even to guess at what they feel and think. I feel.

My journey through life has given me ample opportunities to make contact with people from different walks of life. Invariably, these people are the ones who have been the other travellers on a public or private conveyance, and they have been the most prolific contributors of my various experiences.

I do not need to look to the future or elsewhere to know how happy I feel here and now.

During the Hours of Daylight

I walked anxiously through the corridor of the Watches of Switzerland to pick up a special edition of Breitling MontBrillant 1903, 37/100. I fretted about; my head was heavy, splitting in excitement and a sense of realisation that

I have never known before; I had these incredible thoughts of joy while I held the magnificent piece in my hand.

I believe, I can foresee the consequences of something I have done; the negative memories are the ones I feel first. My thoughts and images at this juncture begin to feel clouded, start distracting. However, I decide to stop agonising and analysing the purpose of my life, to stay with the present feeling of joy.

It is most certainly a real feeling, which is why I would not muck up at this stage. Something told me it was time to invite the attitude of calm for answers. I know that my mind breed's images, I want to be seen, heard and spoken to, which suggests that my thoughts are forever interfering with my daily business.

I realise that happiness is a present attitude, and I believe in the significance of "here and now," not in the future situation.

My struggle with today is that I don't know whether or not that I can replace any of my thoughts or strike off any further breeding images from my mind. My friends and associates used the words, "Chill out, eh!"

Their response was polite and mild with a solution, "Chill out!" Go on a girl's night out or take a holiday away from the family, which to me causes much angst, this solution so worrisome that I let my expressions and changing moods remain submerged.

During this period, almost everyone except me did something similar in the circumstances. What I chose was the idea of running through my experiences and choosing which part of feelings I am going to respond to. I like to express how I feel and think.

I decide not to escape from the present to know how happy I feel "here and now." I feel like acting within the emotional confines of the family politics ; escape is the act that echoes my own self-condemnation; I need to act in the present.

I learned the truth that my friends are simply not me and do not feel or act like me and that is not wrong.

I am always anxious of radical differences between my hopes about the future and the realistic life itself. I feel that my husband is the most amazing person, a man of refreshing candour; I love him and our relationship. He has helped me essentially to recognise my own attributes rather than my limitations only and to feel the facts of life with joy and ease.

As well as being an amazing person, he can be quite annoying too, especially when he rather quickly tries to erase my dark vision of the future through a reasoning process, making me feel that everything will be "okay," that everything can be fixed.

My anxiety does not come from thinking about the future but from wanting it to be free of any politics of family drama. It is the tension between what the future "should be" and what it is that I do not need and cannot endure any longer.

I do not look for trouble, but my problem is that I analyse life and its purpose instead of living it.

The thing that I realised through these many amazing years is that I have determination, integrity and commitment, and these three are not for strikes. My experiences have shown that I can make a difference, and most of all, I like to live in whole, not in part, and I have been through some tough situations with dignity.

I occasionally want to be reunited with some old friends and links from the past. I don't presume even to guess at what I would feel like when I meet those I haven't seen for more than a decade. I guess, I hope that they have had a good life; I also think that grass is greener on the other side, or sometimes the past seems very safe and pleasurable to remember or to talk about.

I am so glad that I am here and I have the opportunity now. Although I don't know what it is that I would be looking for in them, it would be nice to meet someone from that era, someone from the past. I remember the last time that we met, that it was the time, which was not probably meant for parting. Thinking of old friends and family brings back a lot of memories, huge meanings in my life. Some memories come with sharp soreness, and others with rock-solid joy. My life's mission is to feel again and with warmth the missing and the beautiful moments of my life, rather than the expectations.

I most certainly would like to age gracefully with cheerful thoughts and memories. My memories or images of these are just a simple look around going from terrible confusion to happiness within me. In my naivety, I think that everybody would do the right thing. I am at least being hopeful.

If I want to explore my past links, share and express my feelings, then I am acting more like myself by doing it.

I often hear people talking to their friends or family, admitting feeling hurt in their relationships, and others suggesting to them the various and easy ways to prevent possible heart ache and hurt in the future. I admit that I have done the same on so many occasions.

Now, in a rather cynical way, I feel that, like me, they are quite often attempting to secure the area of their own uncertainty and made-up belief that they know exactly what or how the other person is thinking and feeling. If I tried to act sympathetic and give advice, then I won't have to admit to my feelings of hurt.

In trying to be nice and doing good, I do not realise that the potential suffering and danger lies in losing sight of the person who is hurting. It might feel easier to tip up my own life with a little joyful moment of self-importance, or I might feel better, if I can skip the advisory role and remember all those who have done amazing, amazing things. The way I see it that ignorance of one's own experiences is no excuse, and enjoying success or achieving happiness is not some clandestine scheme.

I accept my faults, and I most certainly doubt my feelings of righteousness. This suggests that I am not the way I like to think of myself.

"These people happen to be my own, I would much rather if I had to suffer their pain." I have so often heard people say these words, and on many occasions, I have also randomly made use of such statements. I meant it at the time, but in the real world, I feel myself as continually feeling impotent, due to my inability to feel exactly the same level of pain that someone else might be feeling.

I admit my desire to feel their hurt, but I can only imagine feeling like Max or Maxine, finding that I cannot get any closer to feeling their feelings, whether it is of joy or pain. I kind of like the idea of possessing a special power so I could blend into everyday life at any chance. Nobody can see feeling. The only way for me to feel the other person's feeling is to allow them the experience, not raise questions.

I am afraid that my mind simply cannot know what and how I ought to be feeling.

Something tells me it is time to respond. I still deny and do not want to know what it is that tells me, "What I should do?" Days of fatigue and panic insist and tell me I am not at rest. I can see, I don't like the way I feel unrested. I realise that I have this deep need in me. I so much want to be counted.

All over again, I put myself in the hands of emotional links, especially during all my lows in the life, and silence on their part during these periods seems as revolting as some of their words. "Too bad" I have to go all the way through drags, to talk fair-minded business with my loved ones.

It took me a long time to mull over and comprehend or even begin to differentiate what unease and serenity means to my family or me. I sort of always concealed the rough edged events. I tried waiting for those who cared for me to tilt their manner and acknowledge my being not as anyone but as an individual.

It became clear to me from early years that I have ability to get things done, and it is a combination of two elements: the desire to live with dignity and the capacity to maintain grace under pressure. I am no crusader of how people need to run their lives or maintain stability in relationships. I do not see myself in any way more knowledgeable about the politics of melancholy versus happiness.

I simply feel the feelings. What I feel today may even mean virtually nil tomorrow.

Days of emotional pain and fatigue kept me up many nights and taught me that I am very good at enduring pain. It took a hell of a long time to realise this, to feel at what I felt. I think experience has its rewards; I have had absolutely nothing to do with Mac being a brute and a bully. Last night I proved myself right.

He is a self-righteous hypocrite, and no one can ever say that I went without a fight. Asking myself, "but why?" then do I continue to feel as though I am standing in the street corner with a cup in my hand, always explaining myself. I believe I am never anything but poor in relationships. I have taken care of myself for more than a decade just fine; I would never like to let it come to prove how mean I am too. By spending too much time thinking about Mac's power over me sort of gives the paradoxical effect of making his act seem trivial.

I believe that at this juncture, I am being more than ever as thoughtless as Mac.

I have been naïve, sometimes selfish and self-indulgent; my entire life comes up more like a cloud before my face, desperately trying to feed snippets from the various experiences for thought and reflection. I sit still until sunset.

I try to crack the silent thoughts, finding myself filling in the gaps with new thoughts picked up through my various journeys. I can tell at a glance a "good feeling" and what this means. It would have been better still if the means would let me do the right thing, no matter how determined I am on wanting "to be" and "what I am."

Life is like being on an emotional rollercoaster. As of lately, I don't like what I see in the mirror, and Jean says, she will do everything for me to make me look beautiful. I do not feel fine. My chin is fat, my stomach bulges, and I cannot put anything in my life together. I have too many things to do. Yeah! I feel so confused. I wait for so many dramatic results. I feel more like a real donkey on this earth.

While in a state of complete disorder, I made sure everybody in my family knew that it was I and nobody else, who would be able to tell "who I am."

I obstinately stayed silent. And both my family and associates did not even bother to look me up any longer. I helped the confusion especially by harmonising with everything that the others said or did.

There is no way I could feel betrayed if I did not so badly want us to be close. I am a relationship ever struggling nonetheless.

I do not presume even to guess at what I felt at seeing Erika, at her complete transformation. She walked in with a vibrant smile, with a lip liner tattooed and with large saline filled or silicon breasts. She looked sexy, clued up, and by the looks of it, with a mission to look beautiful.

Erika told me that it cost her more than £20K; she told everyone that she had researched extensively before she decided to make use of the every available mix of beauty treatment. Besides the silicon breasts and lip liner, she also got the eyeliner tattooed, liposuction on chin, liposuction under the arms, liposuction under inner legs, and configuration of the muscles on her stomach.

My thoughts were trying new ways to invite answers, while I was ogling Erika's new looks in wonderment. It began occurring to me that the ability to get things done could be a combination of a number of elements with simply a strong desire to do them and the capacity to celebrate joy and wish to look nice.

Erika told me about the ways in which she grappled with anorexia during adolescent years, that her mother and other family made terrible fun of her, that other children teased her too. She dropped out of education. She came home and would cry, but nobody noticed or looked up to her. She felt so small. Erika waited for years to correct her body through these various surgeries, and she finds her new transformation totally magical and feels so ecstatic.

To get my answers, I have to feel through her and not look at me.

I let it come to the choice of calling up selected memories, both joyful and painful from my various relationships all through. I admit that my memories are not always a good guide to finding ways to resolve any new stuff. I am a relationship ever growing, coping and adapting in the best possible way to all the new stuff that emerges all over again.

Nick thought that he would get Carl into frenzy when he told him that his ex, Emily, was planting scepticism against him. Carl admitted that Emily's behaviour troubled him, but he did not judge his life by relying on her attempts to discredit him. "I will most certainly not go reeling into a roaring rampage of settling of scores," replied Carl.

This suggests that he was able to see her desire to hurt; he acknowledged he would have never let his negative feelings come to the choice of being malicious. I like him especially as he knows about the differences and the two elements such as negative feelings and destructive acts.

Choosing to harbour negative feelings is confining and prevents the desire to live in the present or look to progress and growth.

Dusk

A while back, I set out to my journey of the chitchat initiative and listened in some very interesting short, sharp stories of people on the trains and buses and most recently during my tour to India. I am totally captivated by India, by its beauty, history and, most of all, the courage and the smiling faces of the poverty stricken folks. I learn most about myself by looking at myself in relation to others.

I appreciate the radical differences between the East and the West, and my experiences have shown that there is no such thing as better than the other in a world of differences and individuals.

Meeting people is change; I may be of value to someone today, or vice-versa. I feel immense joy, especially when people talk about new things and all their other affectations of calm amidst the very exciting and expensive or hushed life style.

I see new faces on the high streets, I observe the window shops being decorated on a regular basis, and I wonder about the amazing gossip columns in the magazines, reality television shows or holiday retreats, as well as the general fun and frolic that comes along.

Ever since I can remember, my feelings have been, little

by little, swayed by the daily happenings through chitchat that I listen in to, the way people laugh, express sadness or carry kit and sit across the corner. I wait for any frivolous activity to happen while I pretend to be out of it during my travels to and from work. This drill on a daily basis sort of helps me dump and sometimes alleviate the melancholic thoughts, even suggest what I want.

In the hours between dawn and dusk, I always give myself an opportunity to take a visit to my little town of "hope." I think, it is not naïve to be hopeful. Memories from the past simply call up all over again, and a great deal of mixed trauma and ecstasy absorbs into my head.

It is not the way I see my circumstances but the way I want to see these.

Sights on the trains or any other journeys come with an amazing feel, anticipation. I feel I am living an interesting life, despite the fact that I am simply sharing the various events from a distance and silently.

There are a variety of expressions, joy and warmth coming through somebody else's laughter, more like an active nattering between the two passengers, which takes hold. They talk about reasons how friends can become lovers, and then there is a quick shift concerning the political games and the politicians.

However silly all this might seem, one way or another, these scenes bring into my life momentarily an ultra joyous experience.

Next, I have a peek at the news item in the *Telegraph Newspaper* of another passenger; it reads: "Bankruptcy is like losing virginity; it only pains once." The boredom must be tremendous that I can go through acute phases of amusing myself, realising at first glance that a natter between other people invites ways of being myself, all that is required for answers to my problems. When others say that they are bad at what I believe I am not good at, I like myself better.

I think, therefore happiness is in self-appreciation. I feel like acting.

It would have been better still if the means had existed to make me understand the trickery of the mind no matter how determined I was on doing the wrong and wasting time and energy in analysing the breeding thoughts and images. I learned to give myself to the various relationships from the early childhood years and simply hoped for these to grow and to feel close to them. If Sonny or Hilda or anyone else had a problem, I was willing to take the heat.

I tried to exist as an individual for as long as I can remember. I also tried to piece together a coherent family life. I believed I would resolve the politics within the family. I try, but in reality, that is not easy.

The way I see it, there is no such thing as "perfect" family relationships in the world of individuals.

Memories and links from the past are more like a chip off the old building block, and their feel is electric. Past is knowledge, and it can be rewritten, and the future is new learning. I must therefore be desirous of present, which would allow me, in effect, to live "here and now."

There is too much anger in the world. The way I see it, anger is often an indication of avoiding oneself. I still don't know what it is. I discovered my husband has a knack of watching thoughts, which essentially means experiencing your own thoughts and images and allowing the flow of these, instead of analysing and losing yourself in it. He has a rather original tongue, and I feel "blissful." And that, as I say, is all I will write about him.

The reason is simply that I feel the need to appreciate his support, which is probably what makes me talk just so much about him.

Last month, I received two telephone calls from Sonny and Hilda, wanting me to do things for them. Their attitude and demands could not have been more different on every occasion. My contacts with Sonny and Hilda are often very frustrating. I am afraid of losing our relationship; I meet with them because my experience has shown that life is too short to be apart. I don't like it when they use emotional blackmail.

I need to try new ways of responding so I can see how it is I want to respond. If I feel distressed when responding to their manipulations, then I am the one distressing me. I have never been especially a popular person, but at least I avoided unpopularity. I like to do the maintenance work rather than to do a mop up after a disaster. It is no coincidence; I can choose.

To act in the present is not some clandestine scheme. Joy is a present attitude and not a future choice.

Everyone in my family stopped laughing a long time ago. To care for one another is a casual statement used through the year. With one discord and another, I doubt if they know what matters is not the caring, but the way that one cares. There is a form of ownership in my family; I have struggled intensely for years trying to get through to them in that I am an individual with a need to make my own choices.

Everybody talks, and nobody listens. The politics of my family life is so predictable and acutely melancholic that in order to laugh or to admit joy, I need to keep under wraps my expressions. To have to live my life for my family's approval is more like a sentence, which essentially means continuous frustration and a mucked up life. Today is a dark day for me. Almost to my family, they approve only when I give myself to the relationship, not when I want to act out of concern and respect for myself.

If I let my emotions lean on my family's approval to exist in our relationship, I do not exist.

It was the last day of my work, and I was very ill. I asked my husband, "If I die, whatever might happen to my jewellery." He rubbed his hands together in anticipation, and then without a pause, "I will cremate everything," he said. I burst out laughing. I most certainly was not waiting for him to tell me that he would cremate my belongings.

I believe that my husband's attitude of humour is a profound and needed act of showing care and appreciation; his mischievous mind has interesting twists and turns, and he is always a good cheer. Words of cheer released my anxiety, and these are the ones that echo my self-determination.

I take the desire to live and accept the melancholia and include it in my present. I decide to live "here and now."

Through my journeys on the trains and buses, my experience has shown that many people from diverse groups when they get together seemingly enjoy a chitchat, others gossip or have a little moan about their friends, neighbours, family members and the confused public. I kind of like the idea of listening in on the various views, experiences and talks on melancholy versus happiness.

The same things have happened every week and every day; there have been lots of stories going around, which is why when the dusk descended, I knew that there was compassion for life deep within most of us.

The way for me to live is to add; it's not too late.

Peter loves himself so much, rather in an exceptionally narcissistic and conceited manner. Now, due to his severe disability caused by the medical condition, he spends much of his time at home. I know that he has never really worked for a living and has enjoyed a flamboyant lifestyle from the family's ancestral income. Peter has two very close friends, and they have been visiting his home every day for almost 15 years.

I am struck by Peter's brilliant conceit and the way in which he tells his friends this interesting tale of his achievements and struggles and many ambitious stories about his life. He is so conceited that he'd never believe that someone might ask questions mainly because he knows one of them is profoundly deaf and the other unable to speak.

He sits through for hours on his elaborately handcrafted, very large, double-seated, brass swinging chair. This is most definitely a furniture piece of distinction, intricately decorated with colourful embroidered cushions, and this is situated in a large living room.

Peter also has a great servant, Jess, aged 19. He wobbles because his left leg is shorter than his right leg, which means that he ends up serving his impatient master tea even while he is swinging on his "majestic swinging chair."

Jess has mastered the art of serving tea through an amazing swinging practice and serve part, starting off with the morning task of serving tea and sometimes water and ending up serving Peter faithfully.

I am deeply struck with the radical difference between Peter's grandiose view of himself and a realistic experience of self-love and appreciation.

Mathew, he acts grand! He has an interesting charm. He is vibrant and has a chronic style with swindling words and phrases or what he may have perceived or heard or interpreted as having been said by others. He has splendid stories to tell about his businesses and achievements.

Mathew spins a story to his gain, causes a rift in the routine relationships in a jiffy. He has an ability to cause confusion, being dramatic, and also does not admit to his problems or set about tackling them. He does not pay any attention to the consequences and dire effect of his spin on the routine relationships. He assumes his spins self-destruct and does not even recognise his actions or the relevance.

If I want to express my disappointment in his actions, then I will be acting more like myself by expressing it.

Harriet knows that her husband Ainsley is having an affair with a neighbour. She thinks her neighbour is a very clever woman and describes her as someone with a knack of enticing men.

Harriet justifies Ainsley's affair in that this other woman's seductive ways distracted him, and this is why he is now blatantly asking her to accept their association.

If Harriet does not accept what is, then she won't have to admit that Ainsley is an unfaithful husband.

I am struggling and forever testing my affluent phobia. I recently met two children, Anika and Harry, in Goa (India), and they were between the ages of 8 and 5. They live with their grandmother, Celia, aged 50. They attend school regularly and pass days by talking about their mother.

Celia tells me that their mother is working for a better life for her children and that she works away from home, in Saudi Arabia. The children look happy and vibrant, playing games such as netball and cricket, making impressions in the sand, inviting the guests of the hotel to join them in their game of cricket or netball. Harry especially enjoys story telling and has lots to talk about.

He spoke volumes about his big brother role, how much he enjoys going out and playing with his little sister and particularly protecting her from the horrible sort of big snakes that "hiss" and move around on the beach in the middle of the night. He pointed out to me the way in which these snakes appear from beneath the trees in the great distant green lands.

I guess he was trying to get me to admire his courage. I believe I had to accept his story with a childlike directness, and I think, I did well. He is most certainly a very charming boy. Like Harry, Anika too had charmed most of the guests at the hotel. Both children seemed so tight and very close, always very chatty and full of giggles.

What I am thinking of is, two gregarious, beautiful, happy and extremely cheerful children with a completely confident aura about their life and members of the wider family. They were totally oblivious to the fact of would-be life or the prospects of better life that their mother was striving for.

All in all, I carry from this experience their expressions of deja vu in the present moment "here and now." I opened the door to my mind to the remarkable feelings and activities that Anika and Harry shared with me on a daily basis at the beach.

I was not there to make judgements; I was learning to feel an inextricable state of my thoughts and feelings. It was just too beautiful a time, with nothing to choose between anything.

The way I see it, there is a definitive exquisiteness in poverty, agony and melancholia. There is value and dignity in the endurance of poverty and capacity to survive failure. If I feel I can pull through, I don't have to ask, "What will the future bring about?"

I decide to live now and not think what do I have to do to live a better life tomorrow.

I am standing here in the present. Part of the reason is that I have now discovered within myself a knack for accepting and experiencing the breeding thoughts and images, which essentially means I see now, I feel.

I believe it is invariably the melancholia itself, which is the most prolific contributor that helps explain the many choices and options, attitude of happiness versus melancholy, what it means "here and now."

It is my desire to act in the way that I want, rather than the way I fear. For me, a chapter has closed for today, and for that, I am very, very grateful.

Printed in the United Kingdom
by Lightning Source UK Ltd.
102672UKS00002B/196-363